# M] IN
# IN
# MINUTES

# PARRAGON

First published in 1984
by Orbis Publishing Ltd, London

This edition published 1994 by
Parragon Book Service Ltd
Avonbridge Industrial Estate
Atlantic Road, Avonmouth
Bristol BS11 9QD

Printed and bound in Hong Kong

# CONTENTS

## NOTES

Imperial and metric measurements are not exact equivalents, so follow one set only. Graded measuring spoons are used and measurements are level.

Unless otherwise stated flour is white, oil is vegetable, herbs are fresh and eggs are medium (EEC sizes 4-5). Time for hard boiling and cooling eggs, or defrosting frozen pastry, is not included in preparation time.

To check the temperature of oil for deep frying without a thermometer, drop in a ½in/1cm bread cube. If the oil is the correct temperature (370F/185C) the bread will brown in 55 seconds.

# INTRODUCTION

Conjuring up a satisfying meal when time is short doesn't require a magic wand — just a thoughtfully planned store cupboard and a little imagination. These chapters provide an appetizing choice of nourishing dishes which can be prepared within 30 minutes and are based on readily available ingredients.

Canned foods play an important part when you are cooking in a hurry. The most useful are protein foods — tuna, sardines, salmon, ham, red kidney beans and other pulses — which can provide the basis of a complete dish without too much fuss. Canned tomatoes are invaluable for speedy sauces. When stocking up, choose items which all the family will eat.

A freezer is a great convenience. Best buys are white fish fillets, liver, vegetables and other food which defrosts quickly or can be cooked from frozen. Make the most of commercially prepared food such as breaded fish steaks, fish fingers, pizza and ice cream by dressing them up with a tasty home-made sauce or topping.

Other useful standbys are rice and pasta, which are quick to cook and satisfying to eat, and eggs and cheese which are turned into tasty snacks.

No matter how short the time, always try to include some fresh food in the meal. Cabbage, carrots and celery keep well in the refrigerator and can be swiftly sliced or grated for a crisp salad or briefly stir-fried for a crunchy side dish.

## CLEVER SHORT CUTS

When time is short, quick thinking counts more than Cordon Bleu. Choose a main dish which is a meal in itself — a chunky stew or soup with pasta or potatoes in it — and cook in a flameproof casserole to save on dishing up and washing up.

Stick to simple cooking methods, — grilling and frying are the most speedy. Both require good quality food which cooks evenly, but this can be bacon, sausagemeat and chicken as well as fillets and other expensive cuts of meat.

Make the most of kitchen tools. A blender or food processor will purée soups and sauces, or crumb bread slices in seconds. Raspberries, stoned cherries and other fruit can be puréed, from frozen, with icing sugar and orange juice for an 'instant' dessert sauce.

Forget about fine chopping — roughly slice onions and leave small button mushrooms whole. Snip chives and other herbs with kitchen scissors; scissor-snip cherries and dates, dipping the blades in hot water to prevent them sticking. For a crispy coating for chicken joints or fish fillets, dip the food into beaten egg and then into a breadcrumb stuffing mix. To speed browning, sprinkle sweet paprika over a cheese topping before grilling. Mark butter or block margarine into 1oz/25g before using. This save weighing (or guessing) later.

## COOL CUCUMBER SOUP

1 chicken stock cube
1 cucumber
½ pint/300ml natural
    yoghurt
1 tbls chopped mint
salt
freshly ground black
    pepper
**To garnish:**
mint sprigs
cucumber slices

Dissolve the stock cube in ¼ pint/ 150ml boiling water, then make up to ½ pint/300ml with ice cubes.

Half peel the cucumber, cut it into chunks and place in a blender. Add the yoghurt and blend until smooth. Pour into a bowl, then stir in the stock and chopped mint. Season to taste.

Pour the soup into individual bowls, float mint sprigs on top and garnish with cucumber slices.

**Takes 15 minutes. Serves 4**

## SPEEDY GAZPACHO

1 slice bread
1½ pints/900ml tomato
    juice
2 garlic cloves, crushed
dash of Worcestershire
    sauce
salt
freshly ground black
    pepper
**To serve:**
1 red or green pepper,
    seeded and chopped
1 onion, sliced
black olives
croûtons

Crumble the bread into a blender, then add the tomato juice, garlic, sauce and 2 ice cubes. Season to taste and blend until smooth.

Check the seasoning, then pour the soup into individual bowls. Serve at once, with the pepper, onion, olives and croûtons handed round in small dishes. (Each diner sprinkles some of the accompaniments into their soup.)

**Takes about 15 minutes. Serves 4**

# MINESTRONE IN MINUTES

1oz/25g butter or 1tbls oil
1 onion, chopped
¼ green cabbage, shredded
2oz/50g frozen carrots
2 x 15oz/425g cans
   tomatoes
1 pint/600ml chicken stock
4oz/100g quick-cook
   macaroni
15oz/425g can cannellini
   beans, drained
garlic salt
freshly ground black
   pepper
coarsely chopped parsley
bread sticks, to serve

Melt the butter or heat the oil in a heavy-based saucepan. Add the onion, cabbage and carrots and fry for 3 minutes. Pour in the tomatoes and stock, then bring to the boil.

Add the macaroni and simmer for 15 minutes. Stir in the beans and season to taste, then sprinkle generously with parsley. Serve with bread sticks.
**Takes 25 minutes. Serves 4**

# FRANKFURTER PEA SOUP

1 large onion, chopped
1oz/25g butter or 1tbls oil
1lb/450g frozen peas
1 pint/600ml chicken
   stock
8oz/225g frankfurters
salt
freshly ground black
   pepper
croûtons, to serve

Fry the onion in the butter or oil for 3 minutes. Add peas and stock, bring to the boil and simmer for 2 minutes.

Purée the soup in a blender until smooth, then pour it back into the pan. Cut the frankfurters into chunks and add to the soup. Heat through and season. Serve topped with croûtons.
**Takes 20 minutes. Serves 4**

# TANGY TOMATO SOUP

Fry the onion in the butter or oil for
3 minutes. Stir in the flour, then pour
in the tomatoes and stock. Stir in the
purée, orange zest and juice and bring
to the boil.

Cool the soup for 1-2 minutes, then
purée in a blender until smooth. Return
to the pan and reheat. Season to taste.

Serve the soup in individual bowls,
garnished with orange slices and
watercress sprigs.

**Takes 15 minutes. Serves 4**

1 onion, chopped
1oz/25g butter or 1tbls oil
2tsp plain flour
2 x 15oz/425g cans
  tomatoes
½ pint/300ml chicken
  stock
2tbls tomato purée
grated zest and juice of 2
  oranges
salt
**To garnish:**
orange slices
watercress sprigs

# SARDINE PÂTÉ

2 x 4oz/100g cans
    sardines in oil
salt
freshly ground black
    pepper
grated zest of 1 lemon
lemon juice, to taste
8oz/225g cream cheese
**To garnish:**
lemon slices, halved
parsley
warmed water biscuits,
    to serve

Turn the sardines and their oil into a
mixing bowl, season to taste and mash
well with a fork. Stir in the lemon zest
and juice, then mix in the cream
cheese.

Divide the pâté between 4 ramekin
dishes and smooth each top. Cover and
chill for at least 15 minutes.

Garnish with the lemon slices and
parsley and serve with warm biscuits.
**Takes about 25 minutes. Serves 4**

# TUNA DIP

Turn the tuna and its oil into a mixing bowl. Add the garlic, season to taste and mash well with fork. Stir in the soured cream and half the chives.

Check the seasoning, then turn the dip into a serving bowl. Cover and chill for at least 10 minutes.

Serve the tuna dip sprinkled with the remaining chives, and accompanied with the vegetables and crisps.

**Takes about 30 minutes. Serves 4**

7oz/200g can tuna in oil
1 garlic clove, crushed
salt
freshly ground black
  pepper
¼ pint/150ml soured
  cream
2tbls chopped chives
**To serve:**
fingers of cucumber
carrot sticks
cauliflower florets
potato crisps

# SPICED GOUJONS

4 whiting or plaice fillets
oil, for deep frying
**For the coating:**
2 tbls plain flour
1 tbls garam masala or
    curry powder
½ tsp turmeric
pinch of chilli powder
salt
freshly ground black
    pepper
**To serve:**
1 bunch radishes, sliced
¼ cucumber, sliced
lemon wedges, to garnish

Choose fillets with a light skin and cut them into strips, about ½in/1cm wide.

Mix the coating ingredients in a polythene bag. Add the fish strips and shake the bag gently to coat the fish evenly.

Heat the oil in a deep-fat frier to 370F/185C. Add the fish and fry for about 5 minutes until crisp and golden. Drain the goujons on absorbent paper.

Divide the goujons, sliced radishes and cucumber between 4 individual plates and serve, garnished with lemon wedges.

**Takes about 20 minutes. Serves 4**

# MELON SEAFOOD STARTER

Cut the melon in half and scrape out the seeds. Cut out the flesh using a melon baller or scoop it out and cut into neat bite-sized pieces.

Mix the melon flesh with the onions, pimientos, peeled prawns and oil. Season carefully to taste.

Divide the mixture between 4 glass dishes, cover and chill for at least 10 minutes. Serve, garnished with basil sprigs and whole prawns.
**Takes about 30 minutes. Serves 4**

*1 honeydew melon*
*2 spring onions, chopped*
*6oz/175g can pimientos, drained and chopped*
*8oz/225g peeled prawns*
*2tbls olive oil*
*salt*
*freshly ground black pepper*
**To garnish:**
*basil sprigs*
*whole prawns*

# PRONTO PÂTÉ MUSHROOMS

*12 large button*
  *mushrooms*
*juice of 1 lemon*
*12oz/350g pâté*
**To garnish:**
*orange slices, quartered*
*tomato wedges*
*parsley sprigs*

Cut the stalks from the mushrooms (and save for another use), then place the caps in a heatproof bowl and sprinkle with the lemon juice. Pour in boiling water to cover, leave for 1 minute, then drain and pat dry on absorbent paper.

Fill each mushroom with a little pâté, then divide between 4 small plates. Just before serving, garnish with orange slices, tomato wedges and parsley. **Takes about 10 minutes. Serves 4**

# HOT GARLIC MUSHROOMS

*2oz/50g butter or 2 tbls oil*
*2 garlic cloves, crushed*
*12oz/350g button*
  *mushrooms*
*freshly ground black pepper*
*3tbls chopped parsley*
*lemon wedges, to garnish*
*warm bread or bread sticks,*
  *to serve*

Melt the butter or heat the oil in a large frying pan. Add the garlic, then the mushrooms and cook over medium heat for 2 minutes, until the mushrooms are heated through. Season generously with pepper and stir in the parsley.

Transfer the mushrooms to individual serving plates and garnish with lemon wedges. Serve at once, with warm bread or bread sticks. **Takes about 15 minutes. Serves 4**

# SESAME DIP

*2 x 15oz/425g cans chick-
   peas, drained and
   rinsed
2 tbls sesame seeds
2 tbls lemon juice
2 large garlic cloves,
   crushed
¼ pint/150ml olive oil
salt
freshly ground black
   pepper
lemon wedges, to garnish
warmed pitta bread, to
   serve*

Place the chick-peas in a blender with the sesame seeds, lemon juice and garlic. Blend until the chick-peas are well broken up. Slowly pour in the oil, processing the mixture until an almost smooth paste is formed. Do not over-blend as the dip should have a slightly uneven texture. Season to taste.

Transfer the dip to a serving bowl and garnish with lemon wedges. Serve with slices of warmed pitta bread for dipping.

**Takes about 15 minutes. Serves 4**

# GREEK SALAD

Cut the tomato quarters in half if they are very large. Separate the onion slices into rings and add to the tomatoes with the cucumber and olives. Crumble the cheese coarsely over the top.

Mix the salad lightly together, then transfer to a shallow serving bowl or 4 individual dishes.

Mix the garlic with the oil, season to taste and pour over the salad. Sprinkle with parsley.

Serve with pitta bread.

**Takes about 25 minutes. Serves 4**

4 tomatoes, quartered
1 small red onion, sliced
½ cucumber, cut into chunks
2oz/50g black olives
8oz/225g Feta cheese or Caerphilly cheese
2 garlic cloves, crushed
2tbls olive oil
salt
freshly ground black pepper
chopped parsley, to garnish
warmed pitta bread, to serve

# CURRIED EGGS MAYONNAISE

8 poppadums
oil, for brushing
4 large hard-boiled eggs
2¾oz/70g garlic-
    flavoured full fat soft
    cheese
7fl oz/200ml curried
    mayonnaise
2tbls peach chutney
½tsp curry powder
**To garnish:**
2 red chillies, sliced into
    rings and seeded
coriander sprigs

Brush each poppadum lightly on 1 side with oil. Cook the poppadums, 2 or 3 at a time, under a hot grill for 20-30 seconds on each side until crisp and puffy. Take care that the poppadums are not close to the heat or they will catch fire as they rise. Place on a plate.

Cut the eggs in half, scoop out the yolk and mash with the garlic-flavoured cheese. Spoon the egg yolk mixture back into the egg whites, pressing down well.

Divide the eggs between 4 small plates, placing them cut side down. Blend the mayonnaise with the chutney and curry powder, then spoon over the eggs.

Garnish with chilli rings and coriander. Serve with the poppadums.
**Takes 15-20 minutes. Serves 4**

# GINGER GRAPEFRUIT

Halve the grapefruit. Using a small serrated knife, cut between the membrane and white pith to loosen the segments. Stand the halves, cut side up, on a sheet of foil in the grill pan.

Spoon 1 tbls wine and ½ tbls sugar over each fruit, then grill until hot and lightly browned.

Transfer the fruit to 4 individual plates and top each half with a cherry. Spoon the juices from the grill pan over the grapefruit and serve at once.

**Takes about 20 minutes. Serves 4**

*2 grapefruit*
*4 tbls ginger wine*
*2 tbls demerara sugar*
*4 glacé cherries, cut in half*

# APRICOT APPETIZER

Dry-fry the bacon in a non-stick pan until browned, stirring constantly to prevent sticking. Drain the bacon on absorbent paper and allow to cool.

Add the bacon and chives to the cheese, season to taste and mix thoroughly together. Divide the mixture evenly and neatly between the apricot halves.

Garnish the apricots with the olives and serve on cucumber slices.

**Takes about 20 minutes. Serves 4-6**

*4 oz/100g rindless smoked bacon rashers, chopped*
*1 tbls chopped chives*
*8 oz/225g cream cheese*
*salt*
*freshly ground black pepper*
*15 oz/425g can apricot halves, drained*
*stuffed green olives, sliced, to garnish*
*cucumber slices, to serve*

## MACARONI WITH SALAMI

8oz/225g quick-cook
  macaroni
salt
2tbls olive oil
1 onion, sliced
6oz/175g can pimientos,
  drained and sliced
8oz/225g salami, cut into
  strips
2tbls chopped parsley
freshly ground black
  pepper
grated Parmesan cheese,
  to serve

Cook the macaroni in plenty of boiling salted water for 7-8 minutes, until just tender.

Meanwhile, heat the oil in a saucepan, add the onion and fry gently until soft but not brown. Add the pimientos and salami, mix well and keep warm over very low heat.

Drain the macaroni, then stir into the salami mixture. Add the parsley and season to taste. Serve at once, with a bowl of grated Parmesan cheese.

**Takes about 15 minutes. Serves 4**

## PASTA SUPPER

1lb/450g dried pasta
  shapes
salt
3tbls olive oil or
  2oz/50g butter
2-3 garlic cloves, crushed
freshly ground black
  pepper
4tbls chopped basil or
  mixed herbs
**For the tomato salad:**
1lb/450g small tomatoes,
  quartered
1 small red onion, sliced
  and separated into rings
2tbls French dressing

Cook the pasta in plenty of boiling, salted water for about 15 minutes, until just tender.

Meanwhile, heat the oil or melt the butter in a small saucepan. Add the garlic and cook for a few minutes, then add plenty of seasoning and the herbs. Set aside.

To make the salad, place the tomatoes and onion rings in a dish and spoon over the dressing.

Drain the cooked pasta and turn it into a warmed serving bowl. Pour over the garlic and herb mixture and toss to mix. Serve at once, with the tomato salad.

**Takes about 20 minutes. Serves 4-6**

# TUNA CRISP

7oz/200g.can tuna in oil
1 onion, chopped
1oz/25g plain flour
salt
freshly ground black
 pepper
¾ pint/450ml milk
8oz/225g small button
 mushrooms
2tbls chopped parsley
grated zest of 1 lemon
2 x 1oz/25g packets
 potato crisps
**To garnish:**
lemon slices
parsley sprigs

Drain the oil from the tuna into a heavy-based saucepan. Heat gently, then add the onion and cook for about 3 minutes, until soft but not brown.

Stir in the flour and season lightly.

Away from the heat, stir in the milk. Bring to the boil, stirring. Add the mushrooms, parsley and lemon zest. Flake the tuna, add to the sauce and simmer for 1 minute.

Pour the mixture into a serving dish. Lightly crush the crisps and scatter over the top. Serve at once, garnished with lemon slices and parsley.

**Takes about 30 minutes. Serves 4**

# ITALIAN TUNA SALAD

Drain the oil from the tuna into a small bowl. Add the garlic, capers, parsley and lemon juice. Season to taste and mix well.

Flake the tuna coarsely into a serving bowl. Add the beans and onion rings. Pour over the garlic dressing and toss lightly to mix.

Serve with warm bread or rolls.

**Takes 15 minutes. Serves 4**

2 x 7oz/200g cans tuna in oil
2 garlic cloves, crushed
1 tbls capers, chopped
2 tbls chopped parsley
lemon juice, to taste
salt
freshly ground black pepper
2 x 15oz/425g cans cannellini beans, drained and rinsed
1 small red onion, sliced and separated into rings
warm bread or rolls, to serve

# FAMILY FISH CAKE

4½oz/120g packet instant
  mashed potato
2 x 4oz/100g cans
  sardines in tomato
  sauce
4tbls chopped parsley
garlic salt
freshly ground black
  pepper
**To garnish:**
tomato wedges
lemon slices, halved

Make up the potato following the
instructions on the packet, but using
slightly less water than recommended
to give a stiff consistency.

Mash the sardines with their sauce,
then add to the potato with the parsley.
Season to taste and mix thoroughly.

Line the rack of the grill pan with a
piece of lightly greased foil. Turn the
mixture on to the foil and shape it into
a neat, evenly thick round. Mark the
top with a fork.

Cook the fish cake under a hot grill
until golden brown. Serve at once, cut
into wedges and garnished with the
tomato and lemon slices.

**Takes about 30 minutes. Serves 4-6**

# SMOKED MACKEREL PUFF

4oz/100g chilled or
  defrosted frozen puff
  pastry
2oz/50g butter, melted
2 x 7oz/200g cans
  creamed mushrooms
1lb/450g smoked
  mackerel fillets
2tbls chopped parsley
salt
freshly ground black
  pepper
dash of lemon juice

Roll out the pastry thinly, then cut it
into as many rounds as possible with a
2in/5cm pastry cutter.

Brush the rounds lightly with melted
butter, then arrange on a sheet of foil
on the grill rack. Cook under a hot
grill, allowing plenty of room for rising,
for 1 minute until lightly cooked. Turn
the rounds over and grill for a further
1-2 minutes, until puffed and golden.

Meanwhile, heat the mushrooms in a
small saucepan. Flake the fish off its
skin and remove any bones, then stir
into the mushrooms. Add the parsley
and season to taste. Heat through, then
add the lemon juice.

Transfer the mixture to a warmed
serving dish, top with the pastry puffs
and serve.

**Takes 30 minutes. Serves 4**

# SPICY CHICK-PEAS

Mix the cumin, thyme, chilli powder and garlic salt. Add the chick-peas and mix well to coat.

Heat the oil in a deep-fat frier to 370F/185C. Fry the chick-peas in the hot oil for about 4-5 minutes until golden. Drain on absorbent paper.

Serve warm, sprinkled with coriander if liked, and garnished with lemon slices.

**Takes about 20 minutes. Serves 4**

1tbls ground cumin
¼tsp dried thyme
pinch of chilli powder, or to taste
garlic salt, to taste
15oz/425g can chick-peas, drained and rinsed
oil, for deep frying
chopped coriander leaves (optional)
lemon slices, halved, to garnish

# SAUCY FISH FINGERS

12 fish fingers
oil, for frying
1 onion, chopped
1 garlic clove, crushed
15oz/425g can chopped
  tomatoes
salt
freshly ground black
  pepper
3tbls chopped parsley
2oz/50g stuffed green
  olives, chopped
1 lemon twist, to garnish

Fry the fish fingers in a little oil,
turning them once, until golden.

Meanwhile, heat 1-2tbls oil in a
saucepan. Add the onion and fry
briefly, then add the garlic and cook
until the onion is just soft. Pour in the
tomatoes and season to taste. Stir in the
parsley and bring to the boil.

Arrange the fish fingers on a serving
plate. Pour the sauce over the top and
arrange the olives down the middle.
Garnish with a lemon twist and serve.
**Takes about 20 minutes. Serves 4**

# FRENCH-STYLE FISH FRIES

Heat the oil in a deep-fat frier to 370F/
185C. Cook the scampi, from frozen, in
the hot oil for about 5 minutes or until
crisp and golden. Drain on absorbent
paper.

While the scampi is frying, stir the
garlic into the mayonnaise; season to
taste, then spoon into a small bowl.

Garnish the scampi with lemon
wedges and watercress. Serve at once,
with the garlic mayonnaise.

**Takes about 20 minutes. Serves 4**

*oil, for deep frying*
*1lb/450g frozen breaded*
   *scampi or mixed*
   *seafood*
**For the garlic**
   **mayonnaise:**
*2 garlic cloves, crushed*
*7fl oz/200ml mayonnaise*
*salt*
*freshly ground black*
   *pepper*
**To garnish:**
*lemon wedges*
*watercress sprigs*

# CANNY KEDGEREE

salt
8oz/225g easy-cook rice
1/4tsp turmeric
4 frozen boneless cod
   steaks
1tbls oil
1 onion, chopped
4 hard-boiled eggs,
   quartered
4tbls chopped parsley
freshly ground black
   pepper
lemon wedges, to garnish

Bring 1 pint/600ml salted water to the boil in a large saucepan. Add the rice and turmeric, cover and simmer for 10 minutes.

Lay the cod steaks on top of the rice and simmer, covered, for a further 7-10 minutes until the rice is tender and the fish is cooked.

Just before the fish and rice are ready, heat the oil in a small pan. Add the onion and cook until softened.

Turn the cooked rice and fish into a warmed serving dish. Flake the fish with a fork, then stir in the onion. Add the eggs and parsley and season to taste.

Serve at once, garnished with lemon wedges.

**Takes about 20 minutes. Serves 4**

# SEAFOOD SCRAMBLE

Melt the butter in a non-stick saucepan. Add the milk to the eggs, season to taste and beat lightly, then pour into the pan.

Cook over low heat, stirring constantly, until the eggs are just softly set. Remove from the heat and stir in the tarragon and prawns.

Divide the scramble between 4 warmed serving plates.

Garnish with whole prawns and serve at once, with Melba toast.

**Takes about 15 minutes. Serves 4**

2oz/50g butter
2tbls milk
6 eggs, lightly beaten
salt
freshly ground black
  pepper
2tbls chopped tarragon or
  1tbls dried tarragon
8oz/225g peeled prawns
8 cooked whole prawns,
  to garnish
Melba toast, to serve

# ANCHOVY TOASTS

Beat the anchovy fillets and their oil with the butter until blended, adding plenty of black pepper.

Toast the bread on one side only. Spread the untoasted side of each slice with the anchovy butter, then grill until golden.

Cut into fingers and serve at once, garnished with quartered lemon slices.

**Takes about 10 minutes. Serves 4**

2oz/50g can anchovy
  fillets
3oz/75g butter, softened
freshly ground black
  pepper
4 slices bread, crusts
  removed
lemon slices, quartered,
  to garnish

# SUMMER CHICKEN SALAD

1lb/450g cooked chicken
meat, skinned and
diced
8oz/225g Emmental
cheese, cubed
15oz/425g can peach
slices, drained
1tbls chopped tarragon or
1½tsp dried tarragon
3tbls French dressing
salt
freshly ground black
pepper

Place the chicken meat in a bowl, add
the cheese and peaches and sprinkle
with the tarragon.

Pour the dressing over the salad and
toss lightly to mix. Season to taste,
then transfer to a serving dish.
**Takes about 15 minutes. Serves 4**

# CHICKEN AND RICE LAYER

10oz/275g can condensed
chicken soup
8oz/225g cooked chicken
meat, skinned and cut
into chunks
8oz/225g frozen mixed
vegetables
15oz/425g can cooked
rice
2oz/50g grated cheese
**To garnish:**
2 tomatoes, chopped
chopped parsley

Turn the undiluted soup into a heavy-
based saucepan. Add the chicken and
frozen vegetables and bring slowly to
the boil, stirring.

Meanwhile, cook the rice in 4fl oz/
120ml boiling salted water for
3 minutes.

Transfer the chicken mixture to a
small flameproof serving dish and
spread the rice on top. Sprinkle the
cheese in the centre and cook under a
hot grill until melted.

Garnish with chopped tomatoes and
parsley and serve at once.
**Takes about 30 minutes. Serves 2**

# DUTCH KEBABS

16 pickling onions
2 red or green peppers,
  seeded and cut into
  chunks
2 x 8oz/225g Dutch
  smoked sausages, cut
  into chunks
oil, for brushing
**To serve:**
2oz/50g butter, softened
  or soft margarine
½ French loaf, cut in half
  and split horizontally
crisp lettuce leaves torn
  into pieces

Thread the onions, peppers and
sausages on to 4 metal skewers. Place
the kebabs on a grill rack and brush
lightly with oil. Cook under a hot grill
for about 5 minutes on each side, until
the sausage is well browned.

Meanwhile, butter the bread and top
with the lettuce leaves.

Place a kebab on top of each piece of
bread and serve at once.
**Takes about 20 minutes. Serves 4**

# SPEEDY TOAD-IN-THE-HOLE

Pour the oil into a 1in/2.5cm deep, 7 x 10in/18 x 25cm baking tin.

Arrange the sausages in the tin and cook under a hot grill on one side only for about 5 minutes, or until crisp and brown.

Meanwhile, place the flour and salt in a blender, add the egg and milk and blend until smooth.

Remove the tin from the grill and turn the sausages over so that the uncooked side is uppermost. Pour the batter into the tin, then place the tin over high heat for 30 seconds to cook the bottom of the batter.

Return the tin to the hot grill and cook for about 10 minutes, or until the batter is well puffed and crisp. Garnish and serve at once.

**Takes about 20 minutes. Serves 2-4**

*1 tbls oil*
*8 chipolata sausages*
**For the batter:**
*2oz/50g plain flour*
*pinch of salt*
*1 egg*
*¼ pint/150ml milk*
**To garnish:**
*cucumber slices*
*tomato slices, halved*

# HASTY HASH

2oz/50g butter or 1tbls oil
1 large onion, sliced
2 large potatoes, coarsely
  grated
2 large carrots, coarsely
  grated
¼ green or white cabbage,
  finely shredded
salt
freshly ground black
  pepper
12oz/350g can corned
  beef, cut into chunks
**To garnish:**
tomato slices, halved
chopped parsley

Melt the butter or heat the oil in a
large, shallow, flameproof casserole.
Add the onion, potatoes and carrots
and fry, stirring constantly, for
5 minutes.

   Add the cabbage and season to taste,
then cook for a further 2-3 minutes.
Stir in the corned beef chunks. Using a
fish slice, press the mixture down in the
casserole, then cook without stirring
over fairly high heat until browned
underneath.

   Place the casserole under a hot grill
until the top of the hash is lightly
browned. Remove from the heat and
garnish with tomatoes and parsley.
Serve at once, straight from the dish.
**Takes about 30 minutes. Serves 4**

# BACON AND CABBAGE RISOTTO

Heat the oil in a heavy-based saucepan. Add the bacon and onion and fry until the onion is just soft. Stir in the garlic and season to taste, then add the cabbage.

Cook for 2-3 minutes, then stir in the pimientos and rice. Cover the pan and cook over fairly low heat for 5 minutes or until the rice is hot. Serve at once. **Takes about 20 minutes. Serves 4**

2tbls oil
8oz/225g rindless smoked
  bacon rashers, cut into
  strips
1 large onion, sliced
2 garlic cloves, crushed
salt
freshly ground black
  pepper
1/4 green or white cabbage,
  shredded
6oz/175g can pimientos,
  drained and sliced
2 x 15oz/425g cans
  cooked rice

# FRYING-PAN PIZZA

10oz/280g packet bread
   mix
2tbls olive oil
4tbls tomato purée
2tsp dried oregano
2 garlic cloves, crushed
salt
freshly ground black
   pepper
6oz/175g Mozzarella
   cheese
2oz/50g can anchovies,
   drained
about 10 black olives
**Extra toppings
   (optional):**
100g/4oz salami, sliced
8oz/225g peeled prawns
6oz/175g can pimientos,
   drained and sliced
1tbls capers, chopped
4oz/100g mushrooms,
   sliced
**To serve:**
mixed salad greens
sliced radishes

Place the bread mix in a mixing bowl, add 6½fl oz/ 185ml warm water and mix to a dough. Turn out on to a floured surface and knead for 5 minutes. Roll out the dough to a 10in/25cm round, to fit a large frying pan.

Heat the oil in the pan, add the round of dough and cook over fairly low heat until the dough is half cooked. (The underside should not be brown).

Meanwhile, mix the purée, oregano and garlic and season to taste.

Remove the pan from the heat, turn the dough over and spread the purée mixture over the top. Return pan to medium heat for about 5 minutes to cook the base.

Meanwhile, slice the cheese, cut the anchovies lengthways in half and stone the olives, if preferred.

Arrange any of the optional toppings on the pizza, if using. Top with the cheese, anchovies and olives. Place under a hot grill until the cheese melts. Serve at once, with a small mixed salad.

**Takes 30 minutes. Serves 4-6**

# BAP DUET

Split each bap in half and spread with butter. Top 2 of the halves with the coleslaw, salami and apple. Top the remaining halves with chutney, corned beef and the orange and tomato slices.

Serve the baps on a bed of lettuce and cucumber.

**Takes about 20 minutes. Serves 4**

2 soft baps
3oz/75g butter, softened
2oz/50g coleslaw
4 slices salami
1 dessert apple, cored sliced and quartered
4tbls chutney
4 slices corned beef
2 orange slices, halved
1 tomato, sliced
**To serve:**
lettuce leaves
¼ cucumber, sliced

# RATATOUILLE-BAKED EGGS

2 x 13oz/375g cans
  ratatouille
4 eggs
salt
freshly ground black
  pepper

Gently heat the ratatouille in a small saucepan, then divide between 4 greased ovenproof gratin dishes. Make a hollow in the middle of each portion.

Crack an egg into each hollow and season to taste. Bake in the oven preheated to 400F/200C/Gas 6 for about 10 minutes, or until the eggs are cooked to taste. Serve at once.

**Takes about 25 minutes. Serves 4**

# SPANISH OMELETTE

2oz/50g butter or 1 tbls
  olive oil
1 onion, sliced
6oz/175g can pimientos,
  drained and sliced
1lb/450g cooked potatoes,
  cubed, or canned new
  potatoes, drained
salt
freshly ground black
  pepper
4 eggs, beaten
2 tbls milk
finely chopped parsley, to
  garnish

Melt the butter or heat the oil in a non-stick frying pan. Add the onion and fry until soft but not brown.

Add the pimientos and potatoes. Season to taste, then cook for 2-3 minutes until the potatoes are heated through.

Beat the eggs with the milk and pour into the pan. Cook over medium heat, lifting the sides of the cooked omelette to allow the runny egg to flow underneath, until most of the mixture has set.

Place the pan under a hot grill until the top of the omelette is set. Sprinkle the omelette with parsley, cut into wedges and serve at once.

**Takes about 15 minutes. Serves 4**

# FRENCH BRUNCH

Place the eggs in a shallow bowl. Add the milk and season to taste, then beat lightly together. Dip the bread in the egg mixture, then fry on both sides in a little oil, until golden brown.

Drain on absorbent paper and cut in half into triangles. Serve at once, topped with the sausage and tomato slices and accompanied with the croissants.

**Takes about 15 minutes. Serves 4**

*2 eggs*
*2 tbls milk*
*salt*
*freshly ground black pepper*
*4 slices bread, crusts removed*
*oil, for frying*
**To serve:**
*16 slices garlic sausage*
*2 tomatoes sliced*
*4 croissants, warmed*

# RAVIOLI WITH MUSHROOMS

2oz/50g butter or 1tbls oil
2 garlic cloves, crushed
½tsp dried oregano
salt
freshly ground black
    pepper
4oz/100g button
    mushrooms, halved
2 x 15oz/425g cans
    ravioli in tomato sauce
1tbls grated Parmesan
    cheese
2tbls chopped parsley

Melt the butter or heat the oil in a saucepan. Add the garlic and oregano and season to taste. Add the mushrooms and cook, shaking the pan over high heat, for 2-3 seconds.

Add the ravioli and heat through, then transfer to a shallow flameproof dish or 4 individual gratin dishes. Sprinkle the cheese over the top, then cook under a hot grill for 1-2 minutes until melted and bubbling. Sprinkle with parsley and serve at once.
**Takes about 15 minutes. Serves 4**

# FILLED FRENCH LOAF

1 French loaf
2 x 4½oz/120g packets
    instant mashed potato
6oz/175g grated cheese
1 bunch spring onions,
    chopped
salt
freshly ground black
    pepper
12 rindless bacon rashers
6 tomatoes, quartered
**To garnish:**
watercress sprigs
cucumber slices

Split the loaf in half lengthways and scoop out all the soft crumb to make 2 cases. (Save the crumb for breadcrumbs, or another use.)

Make up the potato following the instructions on the packet. Beat in the cheese and onions and season to taste. Divide the mixture between the bread cases, then place under a hot grill.

Meanwhile, roll up the bacon rashers and thread on to 1 or 2 metal skewers.

Place the rolls under the grill next to the bread cases. Cook until the bacon is crisp and the potato mixture is brown.

Arrange the bacon rolls and tomatoes on top of the potato mixture. Cut into 6 or 12 portions and serve at once, garnished with watercress and cucumber.
**Takes about 30 minutes. Serves 6**

# WHISKY RAREBIT

8oz/225g Caerphilly
  cheese, grated
2tbls milk
1tbls whisky
salt
freshly ground black
  pepper
4 slices bread, crusts
  removed
16 slices ham sausage
1 leek, thinly sliced

Put the cheese, milk and whisky in a mixing bowl and season to taste. Mix thoroughly with a wooden spoon until creamy, or process in a food processor.

Toast the bread on 1 side only. Spread the untoasted sides with the cheese mixture, then cook under a hot grill until golden.

Cut the cooked rarebit into triangles and arrange on a warmed serving dish. Top each piece with ham sausage and leek rings. Serve at once.
**Takes about 15 minutes. Serves 4**

# CRUMPET SPECIAL

4 crumpets
8oz/225g pâté
2tbls chopped fresh herbs
4 slices Emmental cheese
**To garnish:**
cucumber slices
onion rings
orange twists

Cook the underside of the crumpets under a hot grill until crisp. Turn over and spread each with pâté, then sprinkle with herbs and top with a slice of cheese.

Return to the hot grill until the cheese is melted and bubbling.

Garnish with the cucumber, onion and orange twists and serve at once.
**Takes about 10 minutes. Serves 4**

# PEAR AND STILTON SAVOURIES

Toast the bread on one side only. Slice the pears and sprinkle with lemon juice to prevent them turning brown.

Arrange the pear slices diagonally on the untoasted side of the bread. Sprinkle the cheese on top. Cook under a hot grill until the cheese is melted and bubbling.

Garnish with watercress and serve.
**Takes about 15 minutes. Serves 4**

*4 slices bread, crusts removed*
*4 dessert pears, peeled and cored*
*a little lemon juice*
*6oz/175g Stilton cheese, crumbled*
*watercress sprigs, to garnish*

# DANISH ROLLS

4 long crisp rolls
3oz/75g butter, softened,
 or soft margarine
¼ pint/150ml soured
 cream
2tbls creamed horseradish
1tbls dillweed
salt
freshly ground black
 pepper
3 dessert apples,
 quartered, cored and
 sliced
4 rollmop herrings, cut
 into strips
4 gherkins, to garnish

Split the rolls in half from the top, without cutting through the base. Ease open and spread the cut sides with butter.

Mix the soured cream with the horseradish and dill and season to taste.

Reserve a few apple slices. Add the remaining slices to the soured cream dressing with the rollmops. Toss to mix, then divide between the rolls.

Make 3-4 slits along the length of each gherkin and open out to make a fan shape. Garnish the filled rolls with the gherkin fans and reserved apple slices.

**Takes about 20 minutes. Serves 4**

# SESAME SLICES

Roll out the pastry on a lightly floured surface to an oblong measuring 10 x 4in/25 x 10cm. Prick the pastry well with a fork, then transfer to a piece of foil.

Cook the pastry under a hot grill, allowing plenty of room for it to rise, for about 1 minute, until evenly browned and lightly puffed. Lift the foil and invert the pastry on to the grill rack.

Peel off foil and spread uncooked side of the pastry with mustard. Scatter the cheese evenly over the top, then sprinkle with the sesame seeds. Return to the grill until lightly puffed and golden brown.

Cut into slices and garnish with radish slices and parsley. Serve at once.
**Takes about 20 minutes. Serves 4**

4oz/100g chilled or
  defrosted frozen puff
  pastry
wholegrain mustard, to
  taste
2oz/50g Cheddar cheese,
  grated
1tbls sesame seeds
**To garnish:**
radish slices
parsley sprigs

# CHEESE FRITTERS

*4oz/100g plain flour*
*2tsp baking powder*
*a pinch of salt*
*freshly ground black pepper*
*¼tsp dried mixed herbs*
*1tbls chopped chives*
*oil, for deep-frying*
*1lb/450g Edam cheese,*
  *cubed*
*chutney, to serve*
**To garnish:**
*lemon wedges*
*watercress*

Sift the flour, baking powder and salt into a mixing bowl. Season generously with pepper, then stir in the dried herbs and chives. Add 6fl oz/175ml cold water and mix to a stiff batter, adding a little extra water if necessary. Beat well until smooth.

Heat the oil in a deep-fat frier to 370F/185C.

Drop about one-third of the cubes of cheese into the batter, making sure they are thoroughly coated. Lift them out with 2 teaspoons, then fry in the hot oil for about 5 minutes, until crisp and golden. Drain on absorbent paper and keep warm while you coat and fry the remaining batches.

Garnish the fritters with lemon wedges and watercress. Serve at once, with chutney.

**Takes 30 minutes. Serves 4-6**

# CHEDDAR PIE

Melt the butter or heat the oil in a frying pan. Add the onions and fry until soft but not brown.

Meanwhile, make up the potato following the instructions on the packet. Beat in the egg, cheese, fried onions and their cooking juices and the herbs.

Mix thoroughly, then spread the mixture in a flameproof dish, pressing it down well. Smooth the top, then mark it with a fork. Cook under a hot grill until golden.

Top with the tomato and cucumber slices and serve at once.

**Takes about 25 minutes. Serves 4-6**

*2oz/50g butter or 2tbls oil*
*2 onions, sliced*
*4½oz/120g packet instant mashed potato*
*1 egg, beaten*
*6oz/175g Cheddar cheese, grated*
*½tsp dried mixed herbs*
*4 tomatoes, sliced*
*¼ cucumber, sliced*

# MAIN MEALS

## TURKEY RISOTTO

*2oz/50g butter or 2tbls oil*
*1lb/450g uncooked turkey*
*meat, cut into pieces*
*1 onion, chopped*
*2 x 5oz/100g packets*
*savoury rice with mixed*
*vegetables*
*2tbls chopped mixed herbs*
*salt*
*freshly ground black*
*pepper*

Melt the butter or heat the oil in a saucepan. Add the turkey and the onion and fry until the turkey is golden on all sides.

Pour in the rice mixes and add 1½ pints/850ml cold water. Bring to the boil and simmer uncovered for 20 minutes, until the rice is tender.

Remove from the heat and stir in the herbs. Check the seasoning and serve.
**Takes 25 minutes. Serves 4**

## RICH TURKEY RAGOUT

*2tbls oil*
*1lb/450g uncooked turkey*
*meat, cut into chunks*
*12oz/350g mixed frozen*
*small whole onions,*
*baby carrots and cut*
*French beans*
*salt*
*freshly ground black*
*pepper*
*10oz/275g can condensed*
*consommé*
*4oz/100g small button*
*mushrooms*
*15oz/425g can haricot*
*beans, drained and*
*rinsed*
*2tbls chopped parsley*

Heat the oil in a heavy-based saucepan, add the turkey and fry until golden on all sides.

Add the frozen vegetables and fry for a further 2 minutes. Season to taste, then stir in the soup. Bring to the boil and simmer for 5 minutes.

Add the mushrooms and haricot beans and simmer for 1 minute to heat through. Serve hot, sprinkled with parsley.
**Takes 25-30 minutes. Serves 4**

# SEAFOOD CHOWDER

2 x 15oz/425g cans cream
  of onion soup
1lb/450g smoked haddock
  fillets
4-6 scallops, halved
4oz/100g frozen mussels
  or mussels preserved in
  brine
6oz/175g peeled prawns
3tbls chopped parsley
salt
freshly ground black
  pepper
**To serve:**
4 thick slices bread
3oz/75g butter, softened,
  or soft margarine
2 garlic cloves, crushed

Pour the soup into a heavy-based
saucepan and stir over low heat until
warmed through. Cut the haddock into
chunks and remove any bones, then
add to the soup with the scallops.
Simmer gently for 10 minutes.

Add the mussels, prawns and parsley,
season to taste and simmer for 5
minutes, or until the fish and scallops
are cooked.

Meanwhile, toast the bread on 1
side. Beat the butter with the garlic,
then spread over the untoasted side of
the bread. Grill until golden, then cut
each slice in half.

Serve the chowder in individual
bowls, with the garlic bread.

**Takes about 20 minutes. Serves 4**

# GRILLED ALMOND TROUT

Leave the heads on the trout, but cut off the fins.

Line the grill pan with foil and grease it with a little of the butter. Arrange the fish on the foil and dot with the remaining butter. Sprinkle the fish with the lemon juice and season to taste.

Cook the fish under a hot grill for 7-10 minutes on each side, turning once, until the fish is opaque and flakes easily. Do not overcook or the fish will be dry.

Meanwhile, prepare the salad: toss the watercress, chives (if using) and cucumber together in the dressing.

Sprinkle the almonds over the trout, spoon over a little of the buttery juices and grill for a further 1-2 minutes to brown the nuts.

Garnish the fish with lemon slices and parsley and serve at once, with the salad.

**Takes 25-30 minutes. Serves 4**

4 x 8oz/225g trout,
  cleaned
3oz/75g butter
a little lemon juice
salt
freshly ground black
  pepper
2oz/50g flaked almonds
**For the salad:**
2 bunches watercress,
  trimmed
2tbls chopped chives
  (optional)
¼ cucumber, halved
  lengthways and sliced
2tbls French dressing
**To garnish:**
lemon slices
parsley sprigs

# AVOCADO FISH FILLETS

oil, for deep frying
4 breaded plaice, cod or
    haddock fillets
2 ripe avocados
1 lemon
salt
freshly ground black pepper
1 tbls chopped chives
parsley sprigs, to garnish

Heat the oil in a deep-fat frier to 370F/
185C. Fry the fish fillets in the hot oil
for 5 minutes until golden, then drain
on absorbent paper.

Meanwhile, halve, stone and peel
the avocados, then cut into slices. Cut
the lemon in half. Squeeze the juice
from 1 half; slice the remaining lemon,
then cut the slices in half.

Sprinkle the avocado slices with the
lemon juice, season to taste and scatter
the chives on top.

Arrange the fish fillets on a heated
serving plate, top with the avocados
and garnish with lemon slices and
parsley. Serve at once, while the
coating is crisp.

**Takes about 20 minutes. Serves 4**

# PLAICE PLAKI

8 small plaice fillets
2 oz/50g butter
salt
freshly ground black
    pepper
15oz/425g can chopped
    tomatoes
2 garlic cloves, crushed
2 lemons, sliced
chopped parsley, to
    garnish

Arrange the fish fillets in a single layer
in a buttered flameproof dish. Reserve a
little of the butter; dot the rest over the
fish and season to taste. Cook under a
hot grill for 5 minutes.

Meanwhile, heat the tomatoes with
the garlic in a small saucepan. Spoon
the mixture down the middle of the fish
and top with lemon slices. Dot with the
reserved butter and season.

Grill for a further 4-5 minutes, or
until the lemon slices are lightly
browned. Serve at once, garnished with
parsley.

**Takes about 15 minutes. Serves 4**

# WRAPPED FISH KEBABS

Cut each cod steak into quarters. Cut the bacon rashers across in half. Wrap a piece of bacon around each piece of fish.

Thread the wrapped fish, bay leaves and lemon on to 8 metal skewers. Place the kebabs on a grill rack and brush lightly with oil.

Cook under a hot grill for 10 minutes on each side, or until bacon is browned and the fish is cooked. Serve at once.
**Takes about 30 minutes. Serves 4**

*8 frozen boneless cod
    steaks, half thawed
16 rindless bacon rashers
16 bay leaves
2 large lemons, quartered
    and halved
oil, for brushing*

# CHICKEN TIKKA

8 chicken thighs
3 garlic cloves, crushed
2 tbls grated fresh root
    ginger
2 tbls garam masala
pinch of turmeric
¼ pint/150ml natural
    yoghurt
2 tbls oil
salt
freshly ground black
    pepper
**To serve:**
1 lettuce, shredded
½ cucumber, sliced
1 small onion, sliced
lemon wedges, to garnish

Arrange the chicken thighs on a foil-lined grill pan. Mix the garlic, spices, yoghurt and oil together, seasoning to taste, then spread over the chicken.

Cook the chicken under a hot grill for about 10 minutes on each side, until browned and cooked.

Meanwhile, arrange the lettuce, cucumber and onion on a serving dish, or 4 individual plates.

Arrange the chicken on the salad and garnish with lemon wedges. Serve at once.

**Takes about 30 minutes. Serves 4**

# PILAU RICE

Cook the rice with the cardamom, cinnamon and bay leaf in 1 pint/600ml boiling salted water for 15-20 minutes, until tender.

Meanwhile, fry the onion in the oil until golden; drain on absorbent paper and reserve. Add the raisins to the pan, cook for 2-3 minutes and reserve.

When the rice is almost ready, add the raisins to the rice.

Fork half of the onions into the cooked rice. Transfer the rice to a serving dish and top with the remaining onions. Serve at once. This dish is an ideal accompaniment to Chicken Tikka.

**Takes about 15 minutes. Serves 4**

*8oz/225g easy-cook rice*
*3 cardamom pods*
*2 cinnamon sticks*
*1 bay leaf*
*salt*
*1 large onion, sliced*
*2tbls oil*
*2oz/50g seedless raisins*

# CHICKEN TAGLIATELLE

*1lb/450g dried tagliatelle verde*
*salt*
*4 boneless chicken breasts*
*1 tbls oil*
*8oz/225g small button mushrooms*
*10oz/275g can condensed chicken soup*
*3 tbls dry sherry*
*1 tbls chopped parsley*
*freshly ground black pepper*
*sweet paprika, for dusting*

Cook the tagliatelle in plenty of boiling salted water for about 15 minutes, or until just tender.

Meanwhile, cut the chicken into chunks. Heat the oil in a saucepan, add the chicken and fry for about 10 minutes, until golden. Add the mushrooms and toss well, then pour in the soup and bring to the boil. Stir in the sherry and parsley. Season to taste and simmer for 1 minute.

Drain the tagliatelle and transfer to a warmed serving dish. Pour the chicken mixture on top, sprinkle with paprika and serve.

**Takes about 25 minutes. Serves 4**

# CHICKEN TONNATO

Cut the chicken meat into bite-sized pieces and arrange with the cucumber slices on a serving plate.

Turn the tuna and its oil into a bowl and mash well with a fork. Stir in the mayonnaise and soured cream and season to taste.

Spoon the tuna dressing over the chicken. Arrange the pimientos on top and garnish with cucumber slices. Serve with crusty bread or new potatoes.

**Takes about 20 minutes. Serves 4**

*1lb/450g cooked chicken meat, skinned*
*½ cucumber, sliced*
*7oz/200g can tuna in oil*
*¼ pint/150ml mayonnaise*
*¼ pint/150ml soured cream*
*salt*
*freshly ground black pepper*
*6oz/175g can pimientos, drained and sliced*
*cucumber slices, to garnish*
*crusty bread or boiled new potatoes, to serve*

# TASTY PORK THATCH

1 onion, chopped
1lb/450g sausagemeat
8oz/225g frozen diced
  carrots
½tsp dried rubbed sage
pinch of dried thyme
4oz/100g button
  mushrooms, quartered
salt
freshly ground black
  pepper
¼ pint/150ml dry cider
2tbls chopped parsley
4½oz/120g packet instant
  mashed potato
2oz/50g grated cheese
**To garnish:**
tomato slices
parsley sprig

Fry the onion with the sausagemeat in a saucepan, breaking up the sausagemeat as it cooks. When the onion is soft, stir in the carrots, herbs and mushrooms. Season to taste and cook for 2 minutes.

Pour in the cider and add the chopped parsley. Bring to the boil and cook for 2 minutes, then transfer the mixture to a flameproof serving dish or 4 small gratin dishes.

Make up the potato following the instructions on the packet and beat in the cheese. Spread over the top of the sausagemeat mixture, then cook under a hot grill until browned. Garnish with tomato and parsley. Serve at once.
**Takes 30 minutes. Serves 4**

# CHILLI CON CARNE

1tbls oil
2lb/900g minced steak
2 onions, chopped
1-2tbls chilli powder
salt
freshly ground black
  pepper
1 pint/600ml beef stock
2 x 15oz/425g cans red
  kidney beans, drained
  and rinsed
2tbls tomato purée
4tbls chopped parsley
warm French bread, to
  serve

Heat the oil in a flameproof casserole, add the minced steak and onions and fry until browned. Stir in the chilli powder and season to taste, then pour in the stock. Bring to the boil, cover and simmer for 15 minutes.

Stir in the kidney beans and tomato purée and simmer for a further 2 minutes to heat through. Stir in the parsley.

Serve with warm French bread.
**Takes 30 minutes. Serves 4**

# LIVER STROGANOFF

*1lb/450g lamb's liver, cut into strips*
*2 tbls plain flour*
*1 tbls sweet paprika*
*salt*
*freshly ground black pepper*
*2 tbls oil*
*1 onion, sliced*
*4oz/100g rindless bacon rashers, cut into strips*
*2 tbls brandy*
*¼ pint/150ml soured cream*
*chopped parsley, to garnish*

Place the liver in a polythene bag. Add the flour and paprika and season to taste, then shake the bag until the liver is well coated.

Heat the oil in a heavy-based frying pan. Add the onion and bacon and fry until lightly browned, then remove from the pan with a slotted spoon.

Increase the heat to high, add the liver and fry, turning frequently, until well browned. Return the onion and bacon to the pan and pour in the brandy. Cook for 1 minute, then swirl in the soured cream. Serve at once, sprinkled with parsley.

**Takes 25 minutes. Serves 4**

# LEMON RICE

Cook the rice in 1 pint/600ml boiling salted water for 15-20 minutes, until tender.

As soon as the rice is cooked, add the lemon zest and plenty of pepper and mix well with a fork. Check the seasoning.

Turn the rice.into a serving dish, garnish with lemon slices and serve at once.

**Takes about 20 minutes. Serves 4**

8oz/225g easy-cook rice
salt
grated zest of 2 lemons
freshly ground black
    pepper
lemon slices, halved, to
    garnish

# FIVE-HERB RICE

Cook the rice in 1 pint/600ml boiling salted water for 15-20 minutes, until tender.

Just before the rice is cooked, melt the butter in a small saucepan, then stir in the herbs.

Pour the buttery herb mixture over the cooked rice and mix well with a fork. Check the seasoning. Garnish and serve at once.

**Takes about 20 minutes. Serves 4**

8oz/225g easy-cook rice
salt
2oz/50g butter or
    margarine, diced
2tbls chopped chives
2tbls chopped parsley
generous pinch of dried
    thyme
1tsp dried oregano
1tsp chopped mint
freshly ground black
    pepper
mint and thyme sprigs, to
    garnish

# MIXED GRILL KEBABS

8 button mushrooms
4 rindless bacon rashers,
    cut across in half
8 lambs' kidneys, halved
    and cored
4 tomatoes, halved
8 cocktail sausages
8 bay leaves
oil, for brushing
salt
freshly ground black pepper

Wrap each of the mushrooms in a piece of bacon, then thread on to 8 metal skewers with the kidneys, tomatoes, sausages, and bay leaves.

Arrange the kebabs on a grill rack, brush lightly with oil and season to taste. Cook under a hot grill for about 7 minutes on each side until the kidneys and sausages are cooked and browned. Serve the kebabs at once.
**Takes about 25 minutes. Serves 4**

# TUNA SHELLS

Cook the pasta shells in plenty of boiling salted water for 15 minutes, or until just tender.

Meanwhile, drain the oil from the tuna into a saucepan. Add the garlic and cook gently for 1 minute. Flake the tuna and add to the pan with the olives, mushrooms and plenty of pepper. Stir in 2 bay leaves and keep warm over low heat until the pasta is ready.

Drain pasta shells and stir into the tuna mixture. Serve at once, garnished with the remaining bay leaves.

**Takes about 15-20 minutes. Serves 4**

*8oz/225g pasta shells*
*salt*
*2 x 7oz/200g cans tuna in oil*
*1 garlic clove, crushed*
*2oz/50g stuffed green olives, coarsely chopped*
*4oz/100g small button mushrooms*
*freshly ground black pepper*
*4 bay leaves*

# POTATO KHEEMA

1lb/450g minced lamb
1 onion, sliced
2 garlic cloves, crushed
2oz/50g fresh root ginger, grated
1 tbls curry powder
salt
freshly ground black pepper
8oz/225g frozen peas
1¼lb/500g can new potatoes, drained
coriander leaves or parsley, to garnish

Fry the lamb with the onion, garlic and ginger in a non-stick saucepan. (The meat should provide sufficient fat.)

Add the curry powder, ¼ pint/150ml water and season to taste. Bring to the boil and simmer for 5 minutes. Stir in the peas and cook for 2 minutes more. Add the potatoes, cover the pan and simmer for 5 minutes.

Serve hot, garnished with coriander leaves.

**Takes about 30 minutes. Serves 4**

# SPICED LAMB PATTIES

2 garlic cloves, crushed
2 tbls garam masala
4 tbls chopped coriander leaves
1 tbls chopped mint
1lb/450g minced lamb
1 egg, beaten
salt
freshly ground black pepper
oil, for brushing
lemon wedges, to garnish
**For the sauce:**
1 cucumber, chopped
¼ pint/150ml natural yoghurt
mint, to garnish

Combine the garlic, spice, herbs, lamb and egg, mixing well by hand to bind the ingredients firmly together, and season to taste. Divide the mixture into 8 equal pieces and shape into small patties.

Place the patties on the grill rack and brush with oil. Cook under a hot grill for about 4 minutes on each side, turning once, until well browned.

Meanwhile, make the sauce: mix the cucumber with the yoghurt and top with a sprig of mint.

Garnish the patties with lemon wedges and serve with the sauce.

**Takes about 30 minutes. Serves 4**

# HARVEST CHOPS

4 pork chops
1 1/4lb/500g can plums,
   drained, syrup reserved
1 onion, chopped
1oz/25g butter or 1tbls oil
salt
freshly ground black
   pepper

Place the chops on the grill rack and brush with a little of the reserved plum syrup. Cook under a hot grill for about 10 minutes, until well browned.

Meanwhile, fry the onion in the butter or oil until softened. Pour the remaining syrup into the pan and season to taste, then boil for about 5 minutes. Keep warm over low heat.

Baste the chops with some of the syrup sauce. When they are ready, turn over and grill on the other side for about 10 minutes, basting occasionally with the warm syrup sauce.

Add the plums to the sauce and heat through over low heat.

Arrange the chops on a heated serving plate. Using a slotted spoon, add the plums. Spoon over a little of the sauce. Serve the chops at once, with the remaining sauce in a sauceboat.

**Takes about 30 minutes. Serves 4**

# AROMATIC CUTLETS

Place the cutlets in a polythene bag.
Add the herbs, orange zest and season
to taste. Shake the bag until the
cutlets are coated.

Place the herb-coated cutlets on the
grill rack. Cook under a hot grill for
about 8-10 minutes on each side, until
browned and cooked to taste.

Meanwhile, divide the shredded
cabbage, tomatoes and olives between
4 serving plates.

Pour the oil into a small bowl, add
the garlic and season to taste, then
whisk together with a fork. Spoon the
dressing over each salad, then sprinkle
sesame seeds over the top.

Arrange the grilled cutlets on the
salad and serve at once.

**Takes about 30 minutes. Serves 4**

8 lamb cutlets
2 tbls chopped rosemary
1 tsp dried marjoram
grated zest of 1 orange
salt
freshly ground black
 pepper
**To serve:**
½ Chinese cabbage,
 shredded
8oz/225g small tomatoes,
 quartered
2oz/50g black olives
2 tbls olive oil
1 garlic clove, crushed
2 tbls sesame seeds, toasted

# HAM AND VEGETABLE PUFF

10oz/275g can condensed
  celery soup
1½lb/700g cooked ham,
  cut into cubes
1lb/450g frozen broccoli,
  broken into small
  spears
6oz/175g chilled or
  defrosted frozen puff
  pastry
a little melted butter or
  margarine, for brushing

Heat the undiluted soup in a saucepan. Add the ham and frozen broccoli and simmer for 5 minutes. Pour the mixture into a pie dish and set aside.

Reserve a small piece of pastry. Roll out the remaining pastry 1in/2.5cm larger than the top of the dish. Trim ½in/1cm strip from the edge of the pastry. Brush the rim of the dish lightly with water. Press the pastry strip on to the rim of the dish and brush lightly with water.

Place the pastry lid on top of the pie and press the edges down firmly to seal.

Use the reserved pastry to make decorations and arrange on top of the pie. Pinch the edges of the pastry to make an attractive border, then brush the top with a little butter.

Place the pie under a medium-hot grill, leaving plenty of room for the pastry to rise. Cook for 1-2 minutes until puffed and golden brown. Serve at once.

**Takes 30 minutes. Serves 4**

# SUNSHINE SAUSAGE

Cook the sausages under a hot grill for about 3-4 minutes on each side, until well browned.

Meanwhile, cook the pasta in plenty of boiling salted water for 15 minutes, or until just tender. In a separate saucepan, melt the butter over low heat. Add the sweetcorn and beans, cover and cook gently for 5 minutes.

Drain the cooked pasta and turn into a warmed serving dish. Stir in the horseradish and buttery vegetables. Slice the sausages and add to the pasta mixture. Mix well, season to taste, and serve.

**Takes about 20 minutes. Serves 4**

2 x 8oz/225g smoked
   Dutch sausages
8oz/225g pasta shapes
salt
2oz/50g butter or
   margarine
8oz/225g frozen
   sweetcorn
4oz/100g French beans
2tbls creamed horseradish
freshly ground black
   pepper

# PORK AND BEANS

1lb/450g minced pork
1 onion, sliced
salt
freshly ground black
    pepper
½tsp dried rubbed sage
grated zest and juice of 1
    orange
1 pint/600ml dry cider
2 x 15oz/425g cans butter
    beans, drained and
    rinsed
sage leaves, to garnish

Place the pork and onion in a non-stick saucepan. Season to taste and fry until the meat is well browned. (The pork will provide enough fat for cooking.)

Add the sage, orange zest and juice, then pour in the cider. Bring to the boil and simmer for 10 minutes over a high heat. Add the beans and simmer gently for a further 5 minutes.

Serve hot, in individual bowls, garnished with sage.

**Takes about 30 minutes. Serves 4**

# GLAZED GAMMON

Trim the rind off the gammon, then snip the fat around the steaks at regular intervals.

Arrange the steaks in the grill rack and sprinkle with the orange zest and juice. Top each steak with a cinnamon stick, then sprinkle with the sugar.

Cook under a hot grill for 7-8 minutes, basting frequently with the cooking juices. Transfer the cinnamon sticks to the bottom of the grill pan. Turn the steaks over and cook on the other side for 7-8 minutes, basting frequently.

Transfer the steaks to a heated serving dish and spoon over the cooking juices. Garnish with orange slices, the cinnamon sticks and watercress sprigs. Serve at once.

**Takes about 30 minutes. Serves 4**

*4 gammon steaks*
*grated zest and juice of*
*  2 oranges*
*4 cinnamon sticks*
*1 tbls demerara sugar*
**To garnish:**
*orange slices*
*watercress sprigs*

# SPINACH AND EGG MASALA

4tbls oil
1 large onion, chopped
1lb/450g frozen leaf
  spinach
2tsp ground coriander
2tsp ground cumin
salt
freshly ground black
  pepper
2oz/50g fresh root ginger,
  grated
4 garlic cloves, crushed
4 cardamom pods
4tbls tomato purée
½ pint/300ml chicken
  stock
8 hard-boiled eggs
2tbls chopped coriander
  leaves or parsley

Heat 2tbls oil in a frying pan. Add the onion and cook until soft but not brown. Add the spinach, coriander and cumin and season to taste. Cook gently for 2-3 minutes, then keep warm over low heat.

Heat the remaining oil in a saucepan. Add the ginger, garlic and cardamom and fry for 2 minutes. Stir in the tomato purée and stock and bring to the boil. Add the eggs and heat through in the sauce for a few minutes.

Transfer the eggs and sauce to a heated serving dish, then spoon the spinach around the sides. Sprinkle with coriander leaves and serve.
**Takes about 30 minutes. Serves 4**

# INDONESIAN PORK

1tbls oil
1lb/450g lean boneless
  pork, cut into strips
2oz/50g fresh root ginger,
  sliced
2 garlic cloves, crushed
¼tsp chilli powder, or to
  taste
salt
freshly ground black
  pepper
6oz/175g can pimientos,
  drained and sliced
8oz/225g peeled prawns
1 bunch spring onions,
  halved and shredded
  lengthways

Heat the oil in a heavy-based or non stick frying pan. Add the pork and ginger and fry over high heat until the pork is well browned on all sides. Add the garlic and chilli powder, season to taste and cook for 1 minute.

Add the pimientos, prawns and spring onions. Stir briefly over high heat until heated through, but still crisp. Serve at once.
**Takes 20 minutes. Serves 4**

# TARRAGON EGG GRATIN

8oz/225g easy-cook rice
2 leeks, sliced
salt
freshly ground black
    pepper
2oz/50g butter or
    margarine
2tbls plain flour
¾ pint/450ml milk
1 bay leaf
blade of mace
2tbls chopped tarragon or
    1tbls dried tarragon
3oz/75g Lancashire or
    Cheshire cheese, grated
8 hard-boiled eggs
**To garnish:**
chopped parsley
sweet paprika

Place the rice and leeks in a saucepan and season to taste. Pour in 1 pint/600ml water, bring to the boil and simmer for 15-20 minutes, until the rice is tender.

Meanwhile, melt the butter in an non-stick saucepan. Stir in the flour, milk and bay leaf. Season to taste, add the mace and bring to the boil, then simmer for 2 minutes. Remove from the heat and stir in the tarragon and two-thirds of the cheese.

Spoon the cooked rice around the edge of a flameproof serving dish. Place the eggs in the centre. Pour over the sauce, discarding the bay leaf and mace.

Sprinkle the remaining cheese over the sauce and cook under a hot grill until golden. Garnish and serve.
**Takes 30 minutes. Serves 4**

# SWEET 'N' SOUR BURGERS

Cut the sausagemeat into quarters, then shape each portion into a burger. Arrange the burgers and pineapple rings in the bottom of the grill pan.

Blend the tomato purée and vinegar with the reserved pineapple syrup and spoon over the burgers.

Cook the burgers and pineapple rings under a hot grill for about 5-7 minutes on each side, or until the burgers are well browned. Add the pimientos to the pineapple sauce in the grill pan and cook for 1 minute more.

Transfer the burgers and pineapple to a warmed serving dish, then spoon over the sauce. Scatter over the spring onions, then garnish with watercress. Serve at once.

**Takes about 25 minutes. Serves 4**

*1lb/450g sausagemeat*
*12oz/350g can pineapple rings, drained, syrup reserved*
*2tbls tomato purée*
*1tbls red wine vinegar*
*6oz/175g can pimientos, drained and chopped*
*2-3 spring onions, chopped*
*watercress, to garnish*

# HEAVEN AND EARTH

4½oz/120g packet instant
    mashed potato
freshly grated nutmeg
2oz/50g butter or
    margarine
1 onion, sliced
8oz/225g frozen sliced
    apples
salt
freshly ground black
    pepper
2tbls dillweed
watercress sprigs, to
    garnish

Make up the potato following the
instructions on the packet and season
to taste with nutmeg.

Melt most of the butter in a frying
pan, add the onion slices and fry until
soft but not brown. Stir in the frozen
apples and season to taste, then cook
for about 3 minutes or until the apples
are just tender. Remove from the heat
and stir in the dillweed.

Spread half the potato in a
flameproof serving dish and top with
the apple mixture. Spread the rest of
the potato on top. Dot with the
remaining butter and cook under a hot
grill until golden.

Cut into wedges and serve at once,
garnished with watercress.

**Takes about 20 minutes. Serves 4**

# CARAWAY CABBAGE POTATOES

Melt the butter or heat the oil in a large frying pan. Add the onion and fry until soft but not brown. Add the cabbage and caraway seeds and season to taste. Cook, stirring, for 4-5 minutes until the cabbage is tender but still crisp.

Make up the potato following the instructions on the packet, then stir in the hot cabbage mixture. Spoon the mixture into a buttered flameproof dish, spreading it evenly, then cook under a hot grill until golden.

Serve at once, cut into strips and garnished with lemon slices and parsley.

**Takes 15 minutes. Serves 4**

2oz/50g butter or 1 tbls oil
1 onion, chopped
8oz/225g green cabbage, finely shredded
1 tbls caraway seeds
salt
freshly ground black pepper
4½oz/120g packet instant mashed potato
**To garnish:**
lemon slices, quartered
parsley sprigs

# BEETROOT WITH BEANS

8oz/225g frozen French
   beans
salt
2oz/50g butter or
   margarine
1lb/450g ready-cooked
   baby beetroot, halved
freshly ground black
   pepper
2tsp sesame or vegetable
   oil
2tbls sesame seeds

Cook the beans in lightly salted boiling water until just tender, then drain and keep warm.

Melt the butter in a frying pan. Add the beetroot, season to taste and cook gently until heated through. Using a slotted spoon, remove the beetroot from the pan and mix with the beans.

Add the oil to the butter remaining in the pan, then sprinkle in the sesame seeds and stir over medium heat for about 1 minute, or until lightly coloured.

Pour the sesame mixture over the beetroot and beans and serve.

**Takes about 15 minutes. Serves 4**

# CREAMED CORN

Put the butter, flour and milk into a saucepan and whisk together well. Add the sweetcorn and season to taste.

Bring slowly to the boil and cook for 2 minutes, stirring constantly. Lower the heat, stir in the cream, sherry and chopped parsley. Heat through without boiling.

Serve at once, garnished with parsley.

**Takes 15 minutes. Serves 4**

2oz/50g butter or
  margarine, softened
1tbls plain flour
¼ pint/150ml milk
8oz/225g frozen
  sweetcorn
salt
freshly ground black
  pepper
4tbls double cream
1tbls dry sherry
2tbls chopped parsley
parsley sprigs, to garnish

# DESSERTS

## HOT SPICED FRUIT

15oz/425g can peach
  halves
15oz/425g can pear
  halves
2oz/50g seedless raisins
1 cinnamon stick
4 cloves
4tbls rum
cream, to serve (optional)

Place the canned fruit and syrup in a
saucepan. Add the raisins and spices
and cook gently without boiling,
stirring occasionally, for 10 minutes.

Remove from the heat and stir in the
rum. Serve hot, with cream if liked.
Discard the spices before eating.
**Takes about 15 minutes. Serves 4**

## BANANA DELIGHT

4 bananas
8tbls raspberry jam or
  conserve
2 x 15oz/425g cans
  custard
2tbls chopped nuts, to
  decorate

Slice the bananas into 4 individual
heatproof dishes or 1 large heatproof
dish. Spread the jam evenly over the
bananas.

Heat the custard in a small saucepan
without allowing it to boil. Pour the
hot custard over the jammy bananas,
then sprinkle with the nuts. Serve at
once.
**Takes about 15 minutes. Serves 4**

# PISTACHIO ICE CREAM

4oz/100g ground almonds
2oz/50g shelled unsalted
  pistachio nuts, chopped
2tsp rose water
1-1¼ pints/½ litre
  vanilla ice cream

Mix the almonds, pistachios and rose water thoroughly together.

Place the ice cream in a mixing bowl, add the nut mixture and work in with a wooden spoon until evenly blended.

Turn the mixture into a freezerproof container, cover and freeze for at least 20 minutes or until firm.

Cut the ice cream into slices and serve at once.
**Takes about 30 minutes. Serves 4**

# STRAWBERRY SPECIAL

Defrost the frozen strawberries in a warm place for 10 minutes or until half thawed. Place the strawberries in a blender, add the liqueur and work to a slushy purée.

Place the ice cream in a mixing bowl and break it up with a wooden spoon, then quickly work in the icy strawberry mixture. Turn the mixture into a freezerproof container, cover and freeze for at least 15 minutes or until firm.

To serve, scoop the ice cream into glass dishes and top with fresh strawberries, if using.

**Takes about 30 minutes. Serves 4**

*8oz/225g frozen strawberries*
*4tbls orange liqueur*
*1-1¼ pints/½ litre vanilla ice cream*
*fresh strawberries, to decorate (optional)*

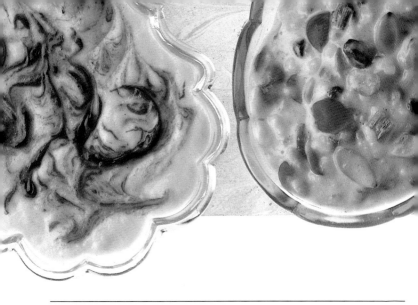

# SEMOLINA SWIRL

2 x 15oz/425g cans
   semolina pudding
7oz/200g jar chocolate
   hazelnut spread
crisp biscuits, to serve

Place the semolina in a freezerproof
mixing bowl, cover and chill in the
freezer for 15 minutes.

Stand the jar of chocolate spread in a
heatproof bowl and pour in enough very
hot water to come half way up the sides
of the jar. Using a knife, stir the spread
in the jar until soft and runny.

Remove the semolina from the
freezer. Pour the chocolate spread over
the top, then lightly swirl it through
the pudding with a large metal spoon.

Divide the pudding between 4 small
serving dishes and serve at once, with
biscuits.

**Takes 20-25 minutes. Serves 4-6**

# RAINBOW RICE

Put the cherries, angelica, raisins and ginger into a small bowl. Add the brandy or sherry and mix well.

Spread the almonds on a baking tray and toast under a hot grill, stirring frequently, for 1 minute or until coloured.

Place the rice in a mixing bowl and stir in the cherry mixture and toasted nuts, mixing well. Pile into individual serving dishes or glasses, cover and chill for 15 minutes before serving.
**Takes about 30 minutes. Serves 4-6**

*2oz/50g glacé cherries, chopped*
*1oz/25g angelica, chopped*
*2oz/50g seedless raisins*
*4 pieces crystallized ginger, chopped*
*2tbls brandy or sweet sherry*
*1oz/25g flaked almonds*
*2 x 15oz/425g cans creamed rice pudding*

# SUNDAE RICE

Place the rice in a mixing bowl. Whip the cream until it stands in soft peaks, then gently fold it through the rice using a large metal spoon.

Spoon the mixture into a serving bowl or 4 individual dishes. Cover and chill for at least 15 minutes.

Just before serving, make a small hollow in the middle of each portion of rice and spoon in the fruit filling. Serve at once, with biscuits if liked.
**Takes 25-30 minutes. Serves 4**

*15oz/425g can creamed rice pudding*
*¼ pint/150ml double cream*
*15oz/425g can fruit pie filling (any flavour)*
*chocolate finger biscuits, to serve (optional)*

# APPLE-BERRY CRISP

12oz/350g frozen apple
  slices
8oz/225g frozen
  raspberries
2oz/50g demerara sugar
2oz/50g cornflakes
2oz/50g toasted skinned
  hazelnuts, chopped
2oz/50g butter or
  margarine, melted

Place the frozen fruit in a saucepan and sprinkle in all but 1 tbls of the sugar. Simmer gently, stirring occasionally, for about 5 minutes or until the apples are soft.

Meanwhile, mix the cornflakes with the reserved sugar and nuts. Pour in the butter and stir well to mix.

Transfer the fruit mixture to a flameproof dish. Sprinkle the nutty cornflake mixture over the top, then cook under a hot grill for about 1 minute until crisp. Serve at once.
**Takes about 10 minutes. Serves 4**

# GINGERED APPLE PUDDING

1 oblong ginger cake
2 pieces crystallized ginger
2oz/50g glacé cherries
8oz/225g frozen apple
  slices
3tbls rum
2oz/50g granulated sugar
cream or custard, to serve

Cut the cake into 8-12 even slices and arrange over the base of an ovenproof serving dish. Cover dish with foil and place in the oven preheated to 425F/220C/Gas 7 for 15 minutes, or until hot.

Meanwhile, slice the ginger and cherries and reserve for decoration.

Place the apples, rum and sugar in a saucepan and cook gently for 5-10 minutes, stirring frequently, until the apples are tender. Keep hot over low heat.

Uncover the cake and spoon the apples over the top, arranging them neatly. Spoon any remaining juices from the pan over the cake to moisten it. Decorate with the ginger and cherries and serve at once, with cream or custard.
**Takes about 20 minutes. Serves 4-6**

# CHEESECAKE FLAN

an 8in/20cm bought
    sponge flan case
grated zest and juice of 1
    orange
1lb/450g cream cheese
4tbls icing sugar
4tbls single cream
juice of 1 lemon
15oz/425g can strawberry
    pie filling
¼ pint/150ml double or
    whipping cream, to
    decorate

Place the flan case on a serving plate and sprinkle a little of the orange juice over the base.

Place the cheese in a mixing bowl with the orange zest, remaining orange juice, the sugar and single cream. Beat together until evenly blended, then stir in the lemon juice.

Spoon the cheese mixture into the flan case and smooth the surface. Pile the pie filling in the centre.

Whip the cream until it stands in soft peaks, then pipe or swirl it around the edges of the flan.

**Takes about 15 minutes. Serves 6**

# TOFFEE-TOPPED FRUIT

Reserve a few of the raspberries for decoration. Mix the apricots with the remaining berries, then spoon into 4 individual flameproof bowls.

Whip the cream until it stands in soft peaks, then spread it over the fruit, making sure the fruit is completely covered. Sprinkle the sugar evenly over the cream, taking it right to the edges of the bowls. Gently press the sugar down with the back of a metal spoon.

Stand bowls on a baking tray, cover and chill in freezer or freezing compartment of the refrigerator for 15 minutes.

Just before serving place the bowls, on the baking tray, under a hot grill for about 2 minutes or until the sugar melts and bubbles. Allow to stand for 1-2 minutes, decorate and serve.
**Takes about 30 minutes. Serves 4**

12oz/350g frozen
  raspberries
15oz/425g can apricot
  halves, drained
½ pint/300ml double or
  whipping cream
6tbls demerara sugar
mint sprigs, to decorate
  (optional)

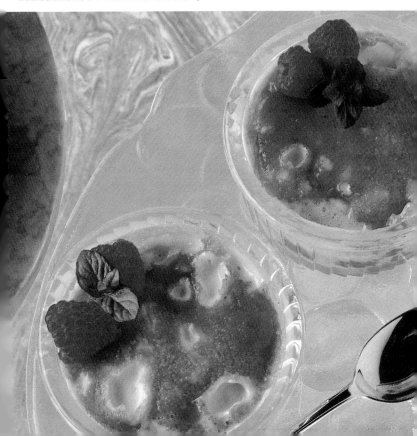

# MARBLED MANGO FOOL

2 x 15oz/425g cans
  mango slices, drained
grated zest of 1 orange
½ pint/300ml double or
  whipping cream
2tbls orange liqueur
orange slices, to decorate

Purée the mangoes with the orange zest in a blender.

Whip the cream with the orange liqueur in a mixing bowl until it stands in soft peaks.

Pour the purée over the cream. Using a large metal spoon, lightly swirl the purée through the cream to give a marbled effect.

Divide the fool between 4-6 serving glasses or bowls, cover and chill for at least 15 minutes. Decorate with orange slices just before serving.

**Takes about 30 minutes. Serves 4-6**

# GINGER SYLLABUB

½ pint/300ml double or
  whipping cream
¼ pint/150ml green
  ginger wine
juice of ½ lemon
1 kiwi fruit
biscuits, to serve
  (optional)

Whip the cream with the wine and lemon juice until it is thick, but not stiff. Divide the mixture between 4-6 stemmed glasses or serving dishes, cover and chill for at least 20 minutes.

Meanwhile, peel the kiwi fruit, cut into slices and cut each slice in half.

Just before serving, arrange the slices of kiwi fruit on top of each syllabub. Serve with biscuits if liked.

**Takes about 30 minutes. Serves 4-6**

# YOGHURT CRUNCH

Place the yoghurt in a mixing bowl and stir in the honey and coconut.

Quarter, core and chop the apples. Reserve a few pieces of apple. Mix the rest with the raisins and orange zest and juice, then stir into the yoghurt.

Divide the mixture between 4 small serving dishes, top with the reserved apple and sprinkle with coconut.
**Takes about 10 minutes. Serves 4**

1 pint/600ml natural
   yoghurt
2tbls runny honey
4tbls desiccated coconut,
   toasted
2 dessert apples
2tbls seedless raisins
grated zest and juice of 1
   orange
extra toasted coconut, to
   decorate

# QUICK CHOCOLATE TRIFLE

1 plain chocolate cake
12oz/350g frozen
   raspberries
4tbls sweet sherry
¼ pint/150ml double
   cream
15oz/425g can custard
**To decorate:**
glacé cherries, quartered
'leaves' of angelica

Crumble the cake into a glass serving bowl. Place the frozen raspberries on top, then sprinkle with sherry, allowing it to soak into the cake.

Whip the cream until it stands in stiff peaks, then fold it into the custard. Swirl the mixture over the raspberries.

Leave the trifle to stand for at least 15 minutes to allow the fruit to thaw, then decorate and serve.

**Takes about 30 minutes. Serves 6**

# CARAMELIZED PINEAPPLE

Drain the pineapple juice into a heavy-based saucepan. Add the sugar and stir over low heat until it has dissolved. Bring quickly to the boil and boil steadily, without stirring, for about 10 minutes or until the syrup turns a pale golden caramel colour.

Meanwhile, cut the pineapple rings into chunks and dry thoroughly on absorbent paper. Thread the chunks on to about 12 wooden skewers and set aside on absorbent paper.

As soon as the syrup is ready, remove the pan from the heat to prevent the caramel overcooking.

Hold the end of a skewer and dip the pineapple in the caramel, turning the skewer so that the chunks are well coated. Hold the skewer above the caramel and allow any excess to run back into the pan, then place on a serving plate.

Coat the remaining pineapple in the caramel in same way. Press a cherry on to the tip of each skewer and serve.
**Takes about 25 minutes. Serves 4**

*12oz/350g can pineapple rings, in natural juice*
*6oz/175g granulated sugar*
*about 12 cocktail cherries*

# EXOTIC FRUIT SALAD

8oz/225g can lychees
12oz/350g can mango
  slices
grated zest and juice of 2
  oranges
2 kiwi fruit, peeled
coconut cookies, to serve
  (optional)

Place the canned fruit with their syrup or juice in a serving bowl. Add the orange zest and juice and mix well. Cover and chill for at least 20 minutes.

Just before serving, peel and slice the kiwi fruit and stir into the chilled fruit. Serve, with cookies if liked.
**Takes about 25 minutes. Serves 4**

# BANANA FRITTERS

2oz/50g plain flour
2 eggs, separated
4oz/100g granulated
  sugar
oil, for deep frying
4 bananas, peeled
2tbls sesame seeds

Sift the flour into a mixing bowl and make a well in the centre. Add the egg yolks and 2tbls water, then beat together to make a smooth batter.

Put the sugar into a small, heavy-based saucepan with 2fl oz/50ml water. Stir over a low heat until the sugar has dissolved. Bring quickly to the boil and boil steadily, without stirring, for about 10 minutes or until the syrup turns a golden caramel colour. Remove the pan from the heat at once to prevent the caramel overcooking.

Heat the oil in a deep-fat frier to 370F/185C.

Whisk the egg whites until stiff, then fold them into the batter.

Peel the bananas and cut each across in half. Dip each piece in the batter, coating it completely. Fry the battered bananas in the hot oil for about 5 minutes, or until golden and crisp. Drain on absorbent paper, then place on a heatproof serving dish.

Pour the caramel over the bananas, sprinkle with sesame seeds and serve.
**Takes about 20 minutes. Serves 4**

# INDEX